MARKEDNESS RELATIONS IN THE PRONUNCIATION
OF THE PREFIXED PARTICLES IN MODERN HEBREW*

by

Ora Rodrigue Schwarzwald

Bar-Ilan University, Israel

Analysis of the pronunciation of the prefixed particles in Hebrew
formal and semi-formal speech shows that deviations from the
norms are of significance only in the minority of the forms, espe-
cially in the rare environments. The findings are explained by a
markedness theory which incorporates frequency and naturalness of
rules and conditions from phonetic, morphophonemic, and morphosyntactic points of view. The pronunciation of the prefixed particles
may serve as a parameter for linguistic registers.

Table of Contents

*This research was supported in part by a grant from the Research Authority at Bar Ilan University, Ramat
Gan, Israel. I would like to thank Profs. Sh. Morag and M.Z. Kaddari for their valuable comments, and
Zehava Saadon, Malka David and Ahuva Yemini for their help in collecting part of the data.

1. FOREWORD

The morphophonemics of Modern Hebrew is based mainly on Biblical Hebrew (BH).
BH set the norms for the correct grammatical formation of the words. These norms
are taught in schools as the proper standard language, and deviations from it are considered as errors which should be eliminated. However, today is Hebrew phonology
not identical to BH. Therefore, changes in morphophonemic realizations ought to be
expected.

The present study is limited to the pronunciation of the prefixed particles in Con-
temporary Modern Hebrew (MH). The purpose of the study is to compare the pronunciation of the prefixed particles to the normative standard rules. The data obtained in
formal and semi-formal speech, show that the prefixed particles are generally pronounced in accordance with normative standards. Deviations are explained in terms of
marked-unmarked relations. It seems that the pronunciation of the prefixed particles
can serve as an indicator for linguistic registers in Spoken Hebrew.

2. INTRODUCTION

2.1 The Prefixed Particles

In Hebrew, four prepositions are prefixed: *bə*- 'in, with', *lə*- 'to', *kə* - 'as', *mi*- 'from',
as well as the conjunctions *və* - 'and', *še*- 'that', and the definite article *ha*- 'the'

which sometimes serves as a relative pronoun (like *še-*). Grammarians in the Middle Ages used the mnemonic phrase *mošeh wǝkaleb* 'Moses and Kaleb' to refer to this group of prefixed particles, i.e., the "servile" letters *m, š, h,*[1] *w,*[2] *k, l, b.* It is this group of particles which will concern us in the present study.

These prefixed particles constitute a special category. In writing, they are attached to the word which they precede. From a morphosyntactic point of view, *bǝ-, kǝ-, lǝ-, mi-, ha-* must precede a noun: *še-* and *vǝ-* may precede any morpheme - nominal, verbal or other. They resemble the particles *bǝtox* 'in(side)', *kǝmo* 'like', *'el* 'to(ward)', *min* 'from', *'ašer* 'that' in meaning, but there are certain constraints on their usage. For instance, *min* may only precede a definite noun,[3] whereas *mi-* has no such restriction (though it becomes *me-* before the definite article) (e.g., *min ha'arec - meha'arec* 'from the country', but **min yisra'el* 'from Israel'). *'el* and *lǝ-* are not always interchangeable: in certain contexts only one of them can be selected, while in others, there is a free variation. Compare the following examples:

1. (a) *halaxti labayit*
   (b) *halaxti 'el habayit*   'I went to the house'

2. (a) *halaxti 'elav*
   (b) **halaxti lo*   'I went to him'

3. (a) *natati lo sefer*
   (b) **natati 'elav sefer*   'I gave him a book'

In the first example, of directional locative, both *lǝ-* (*la-* with the definite article) and *'el* are acceptable. In the second, with a human target, only *'el* is acceptable, as in (2a), whereas in the third example, a case of dative, only *lǝ-* (*lo-* 'to him') is correct, as in (3a).[4]

From the morphophonemic point of view, they are also distinct from the other particles. According to the Biblical and normative grammar of Hebrew, as taught in the schools, the vocalization of the prefixed particles, and consequently their pronunciation, varies depending on the environment which they precede. The other independent particles, such as *bǝtox, 'el,* etc., do not change, regardless of the phonological environment.

2.2 Morphophonemic Alternations within the Prefixed Particles

Table 1 summarizes the morphophonemic alterations which occur in each of the particles, with respect to the environment. The numbers marked next to the forms refer to the comments in 2.2.1.

---

[1] There is another prefixed particle, the interrogative particle *ha-:* It will not be discussed here because of its complete absence in all of the recordings.
[2] The letter <*w*> is pronounced *v* in Modern Hebrew.
[3] With a definite article.
[4] The same is true for other syntactic differences between the independent and the bound particles, and see Berman's (1978, pp. 119-127) discussion.

TABLE 1

THE REALIZATION OF THE PREFIXED PARTICLES
ACCORDING TO THE NORMATIVE GRAMMAR[5]

	ENVIRONMENT - i.e., preceding . . .				
MEANING	CONSONANT CLUSTER(1)	GUTTURAL (2)	yə(3)	STRESSED SYLLABLE	ELSEWHERE
	A	B	C	D	E
'in'	bi-(4)	ba- be- bo-(5)	bī-(6)	_(7)[6]	bə-(3)(4)
'to'	li-(4)	la- le- lo-(5)	lī-(6)	iā-(8)	lə-(3)(4)
'as'	ki-(4)	ka- ke- ko-(5)	kī-(6)	_(7)	kə-(3)(4)
'from'	_(7)	mē-(9)	mī-(6)	_(7)	mi-C (10)
'the'	_(7)	he-(11) hā-(8) ha-(12)	_(7)	_(7)	ha-C (10)
'that'	_(7)	še-(9)(11)	_(7)	_(7)	še-C (10)
'and'	u-(4)(13)	va- ve- vo-(5)	vī-(6)	vā-(8)	və-(3)(4)

2.2.1 Comments

1. The environment, labelled "Preceding a consonant cluster . . ." includes (a) in BH, a consonant (C) followed by a shewa and another C; (b) in MH, a consonant cluster (CC) or a sequence of CeC, where the e stands for shewa. Both in BH and MH, the shewa (or the e) is deleted after the prefixation of the particles.

2. The "gutturals" include both the pure gutturals ' and h, the pharyngeals ' and ḥ,[7] and the consonant r. The r is considered a guttural only with respect to gemination.

3. The shewa vowel sign, ə, is brought here because of the close linkage to the BH vocalization system. In MH, the shewa is pronounced as a mid-front vowel e ((see comment (1) above)).

4. The stops p b t d k g changed in the BH to the spirants f v θ ð x ɣ. In MH only p b k are spirantized into f v x in these environments.

5. Before the gutturals which are vocalized with ḥaṭaf-pataḥ, ḥaṭaf-segol, or ḥaṭaf-qamats, i.e. the compound 'shewas': ă, ĕ and ŏ, the prefixed particles are vocalized with a, e, or o, respectively.

6. Before a yə-, the prefixed vowel is a long ī and the shewa is deleted.

7. The dash means that there is no morphophonemic alternation in this environment. The pronunciation is as in "elsewhere".

[5] Based on BH. For details see Gesenius (1910, pp. 110-112, 298-300, 306-307), and Gottstein, Lievne & Span (1954, pp. 21-27).
[6] The prefixed particles bə-, kə-, və- before the demonstrative pronouns also take a long ā, e.g., bāze, kāzot, etc.
[7] The /ḥ/ is pronounced as x by most speakers of MH. Only one of the subjects had a pharyngeal ḥ. For convenience I use the letter ḥ to refer to the "ḥet" in orthography.

8.   The sign *ā* refers to the *qamats*. In MH it is pronounced as a non-long low central vowel *a*.

9.   The *dagesh* is not inserted in the gutturals and is not pronounced as geminate in MH (see comment (2)).

10. In MH it can be recognized only in the stops *p b k* which are not spirantized (see comment (4)).

11. The *e* reflects the *segol* in the BH vowel system. It is pronounced as a plain *e* in MH.

12. The *he-* occurs before *hā, 'ā , ḥā,* and *ḥŏ*; *hā-* occurs before ', ', *r,* and *ha-* before *h,ḥ.*

13. The vowel *u* also occurs before the labial consonants *p b m v* (=*w*).

2.2.2 Examples

Table 2 presents examples of the morphophonemic alternations in each particle in BH and formal MH.

2.3 Goals

In the present study we will examine the actual pronunciation of these particles by various speakers. We will describe the pronunciation, particularly with respect to the deviations from the normative-formal standards as presented in Tables 1 and 2, and attempt to explain the phenomena involved.

3. METHOD

3.1 Corpus

The data were obtained from the following sources: (a) recordings from radio and television programs from 1976 to 1978; (b) a recording of a paragraph read aloud in 1973: (c) a vocalization of the same paragraph by students, done in 1978.

3.2 Subjects

The subjects included four radio announcers who read eleven newscasts; four television announcers who read twelve newscasts; ten journalists who participated in six 15-minute-long group discussions; ten television reporters who presented local broadcasts from the scenes of events; 39 radio reporters; ten members of the Knesset reading short speeches; eight university students[8] who quickly read aloud a short

---

[8]None of the students who participated had linguistic backgrounds. They were not students of linguistics, nor were they Hebrew language majors.

TABLE 2

EXAMPLES OF THE REALIZATION OF PREFIXED PARTICLES IN BH AND FORMAL MH (FMH)

	ENVIRONMENT									
	A		B		C		D		E	
	BH	FMH	BH	FMH	BH	FMH	BH	FMH	BH	FMH
	bivrāxā	*bivraxa*	*bo'ŏniyyā*	*bo'oniya*	*bīhūðā*	*bihuda*			*bəxol*	*bexol*
gloss	with blessing		'in a boat'		'in Judea'				'in every'	
	lixsūθ	*lixsut*	*le'ĕmunā*	*le'emuna*	*līrušālayim*	*lirušalayim*	*lāqum*	*lakum*	*ləfo*	*lefo*
gloss	'for cover'		'for faith'		'to Jerusalem'		'to wake up'		'(to) here'	
	kilvav	*kilvav*	*kaḥămor*	*kaḥamor*	*kīmē*	*kime*			*kəθof*	*ketof*
gloss	'as the heart of'		'as a donkey'		'as the days of'				'as a drum'	
			mērāḥoq	*meraḥok*	*mīhūðā*	*mihuda*			*mippo*	*mipo*
gloss			'from a distance'		'from Judea'				'from here'	
			hā'ăðām	*ha'adam*					*habbayiθ*	*habayit*
			'the man'						'the house'	
			hahēð	*hahed*						
			'the echo'							
			hehāðār	*hehadar*						
			'the glow'							
			šehāyā	*šehaya*					*šemmillē*	*šemile*
gloss			'that was'						'that filled'	
	uṣdāqā	*ucdaka*	*wa'ăni*	*va'ani*	*wīhūðā*	*vihuda*	*wāḥoref*	*vaḥoref*	*wəšuv*	*vešuv*
gloss	'and charity'		'and I'		'and Judea'		'and winter'		'and again'	
	ufo	*ufo*	*wo'ŏniyyā*	*vo'oniya*						
gloss	'and here'		'and a boat'							

made-up story about Mrs. Regev, a housewife; sixteen university students who were instructed to insert vowels in the same short story. The latter were told to ignore differences of both *pataḥ/qamats/ḥataf-qamats* and *tsere-segol/shewa/ḥataf-segol*, and to mark *dagesh* only in *p b k*. They were assured that the test would examine their pronunciation rather than their knowledge of the vocalization system, and were asked to be as honest as possible. Eight of them did the test twice, before and after a class session.

3.3 Analysis

The recordings were examined carefully. All of the examples with prefixed particles were selected for each speaker and were classified according to the pronunciation, as normative or deviant performance. The pronunciation of the shewa as *e* was not considered deviant. Vowel length was also ignored in the analyses.

4. RESULTS

4.1 Narrowing the Corpus

The results presented below are based mainly on the recordings made from the radio and television broadcasts. This is because:

(a) the results obtained from the groups who read and vocalized the assigned paragraph were found to be consistent with the other results with respect to the deviations,[9] and

(b) since there were only 75 relevant arbitrary selected examples, which constitute a very small and biased sample compared with the thousands of neutral examples obtained from the other sources, it was decided not to include them in the statistical analyses.

A few examples from these groups will be brought forward as evidence.

4.2 Rate of Deviations

The rate of deviations from the formal grammar is relatively small. The percentage of "errors" made by the subjects was as follows:

Radio announcers:	2%	Television announcers:	4%
Radio reporters:	4%	Television reporters:	5%
Knesset members:	6%	Journalists:	9%

---

[9]In spite of the request for honesty in vocalizing the paragraph, the results should be analysed with caution for two reasons: (a) there is no doubt that the writing of the work must have influenced the results, because people tend to be more formal in writing than in speech, and (b) many of the *dagesh* signs were not put where they are obviously necessary, e.g., *banim* 'sons.' They were also probably unintentionally forgotten following some of the prefixed particles.

We see from this that the announcers are much more formal in their speech than are the reporters. The members of the Knesset, as well as the journalists were less formal, that is, they had the greatest amount of deviations from the formal alternations presented in Tables 1 and 2.

4.3 Proportion of Deviations

These figures should be considered in the proper perspective. The deviations almost never occurred in the "elsewhere" environment, which is considered the basic, unmarked form. In this environment (E in Tables 1 and 2), the deviations were primarily related to the spirantization phenomena, e.g., *bepekin* 'in Peking,' *vekaragil* 'and as usual,' for *vexaragil, vekelev, veketem* 'and a dog, and a spot,' for *vexelev, vexetem, lepikuah* 'to a control,' for *lefikuah* (see 4, 4B below). Also, *bediyuk* 'exactly' was pronounced as *bidiyuk* or *bidyuk*, which is already the commonly accepted pronunciation. The particle "from" in the "elsewhere" environment was rarely pronounced as *me-* rather than as *mi-*[10] e.g., *memilyon, mepe'il, mebituim, melemala* 'from a million, from an active, from expressions, from above,' for *mimilyon, mip'il, mibituyim, milema'la.* On the whole, the deviations in the "elsewhere" environment amounted to less than 1%, which is less than 0.5% of all the deviations.

The "elsewhere" environment constituted about 70% of the words. Only 30% of the words belonged to the other environments (A, B, C, and D in Table 1). The percentages presented above (secton 4.2), regarding the ratio or errors, refer to all of the examples. In light of the present discussion, it is obvious that the rate of errors in the other environments is much greater than in the "elsewhere" environment. For instance, in the case of *bə-* ("in"), the television reporters displayed five deviations and two correct pronunciations in environment C (before *yə*). Compare *bidey, bidehem* 'in the hands of, in their hands' vs. *biyehuda, biyerušalaim, beyešivat* (x2), *biyexolti* 'in Judea, in Jerusalem, in the meeting of, in my power,' for *bihuda, birušalayim, bišivat, bixolti.* Thus, the numbers of deviations exceed the number of normative pronunciations in this environment.

In each of the other environments the total number of occurrences is small, and the number of deviations is relatively high,[11] although not as extreme as in the case presented above.

4.4 Types of Deviations

The deviations are of three types:

A.   The vowel which was supposed to have occurred in a specific environment is indiscriminately replaced by the vowel of the "elsewhere" environment, e.g., *behaxana*

---

[10] The tendency is towards the vowel *e*, as in the other prepositional particles.
[11] Commonly used expressions had the least deviations. Form which are heard quite frequently on the radio and on television were rarely mistaken compare: *vešlošim* 'and thirty' vs. *ḥameš ušlošim* 'five thirty,' *bešmona mikrim* 'in eight cases' vs. *bišmone ba'erev* 'at eight o'clock in the evening.'

'in preparation,' for *bahaxana,* (environment B), *lemetula* 'to Metula,' for *limtula* (environment A), *miḥiduš* 'from renewal,' for *meḥiduš* (environment B), *vehamiša, lehamiša* 'and five (m), to five,' for *vahamiša, lahamiša* (environment B), *veleyeladaha* 'and to her children,' for *veliladeha* (environment C), *haḥatul* 'the cat' for *heḥatul* (environment B), etc.

B.   The prefixed particle does not affect the basic word.[12] On the one hand, the consonants *p b k* are not spirantized following a vowel when necessary, e.g., *bepekin, vekaragil, vekelev, veketem* (see section 4.2, above), *ubeikar, lebaala, ulbet-sefer* 'and mainly, to her husband, and to school,' for *uv'ikar, leva'ala, ulvet-sefer.* On the other hand, the shewa in environments A and C is not deleted, e.g., *limetula, miyehuda* 'to Metula, from Judea,' for *limtula, mihuda.* Further examples are presented in section 4.3, above.

C.   The vowel is completely deleted, due to fast speech, e.g., *petaḥtikva* 'in Petah Tiqva,' for *befetaḥ tikva, šḥaverim* 'that friends,' for *šeḥaverim), liybuš* 'to drying,' for *leyibuš, binyan* 'in case of,' for *be'inyan, fhem* 'and they,' for *vehem, šamemšala* 'that the government,' for *šehamemšala.*[13]

4.5 Differences among the Particles

The fewest deviations occurred in *ha-* and *še-*; *mi* had a fairly low rate of deviations, whereas *bə-, kə-, lə-, və-* had higher rates. The rates vary among the subjects. The following list presents the deviations within each group of subjects, in decreasing order of frequency of occurrence. In all cases these represent more deviations than in the usage of *ha-, še-,* and *mi-.*

Radio announcers:	*və-, bə-, lə-, kə-*
Television announcers:	*lə-, bə-, və-, kə-*
Radio reporters:	*bə-, kə-, lə-, və-*
Television reporters:	*və-, kə-, bə-, lə-*
Knesset members:	*kə-, və-, bə-, lə-*
Journalists:	*və-, kə-, lə-, bə-*

In the following sections we will explain these findings.

5. DISCUSSION: MARKED AND UNMARKED RELATIONS

The results presented in section 4 are well-known to every language teacher who tries to properly utter and teach the normative rules of pronunciation. We are not concerned here with the question of whether the deviations should be accepted as new norms, or whether they should be uprooted. Rather, the deviations themselves, as linguistic phenomena, are of interest.

---

[12] See comments (1), (4) and (6) following Table 1.
[13] This type of deviation, interesting as it is, will not be further investigated in this study. Fast-speech phenomena are subject to a more thorough study concerning not only prefixed particles, but all types of morphemes. See Bolozky (1977).

The results can be explained within the context of the markedness theory. We claim that the unmarked forms are those which are the simplest, the most frequent and natural, and therefore, the other marked forms tend to neutralize with them.

5.1 Frequency

The rate of errors, according to the normative criterion, is relatively small. Most of the utterances which include the prefixed particles were properly pronounced according to the base forms presented in column E in Table 1 (the "elsewhere" environment). This conclusion is due to the fact that most of the words used did not have the phonological environment for the changes expected in columns A, B, C, and D of Table 1. Hence, considering the frequency of usage of forms (see section 4.3), the correct pronunciation is unmarked.

5.2 Naturalness Vs. Complexity of the Morphological Rules

The number of words which fit the phonological environment for the changes expected was relatively small. It was primarily in these words that the errors occurred. Considering naturalness in phonological terms, the result is not surprising. The rule formulated for the basic pronunciation is less complicated than the other rules. For example, for *və-* ("and") the basic rule is:

> (R1)   The prefixed particle "and" is pronounced as *və-* (=*ve*),
> and initial *p b k*[14] change into *f v x*, respectively.

The second rule should be stated as follows:

> (R2)   The prefixed particle "and" should be pronounced as *u-*
> when preceding *p b v m*, before a consonant cluster CC,
> or before a word starting with C*e*C, where the *e* stands
> for an original shewa, and that *e* is dropped - and
> *p b k*[15] change into *f v x*, respectively.

According to this rule, /*və+ke'ev*/ → *ux'ev* 'and pain,' from BH *kə'ev*, but /*ve+ke'ur*/ → *vexe'ur* 'and ugliness,' from *ke'ur).*

The next rule for "and" is no less complicated:

> (R3)   Pronounce the "and" as *va-, ve-, vo-* when preceding a
> "guttural" with *ă, ĕ, ŏ* which is an original compound shewa.

E.g., *vo'oniya* 'and a ship,' from BH *'ŏniyya,* but *ve'oni* 'and poverty,' from *'oni;* *va'ani* 'and I,' from BH *'ăni,* but *ve'ani* 'and poor,' from *'āni.* However, the final rule states that:

> (R4)   The "and" is pronounced as *vi-* in front of *ye,* where the *e* stands
> for a shewa.

---

[14] Orthographic *kaf* and not *qof.*
[15] See footnote 14.

E.g., *viladim* 'and children,' from BH *yəladim,* but *veyenan* 'and a winemaker,' from *yenan.* [16]

The same complications could be demonstrated with respect to all the other prefixed particles in which the rules that change the unmarked forms (in the "elsewhere" environment) require more features and more specific environments than the base rule. Therefore, these rules and the subsequent pronunciations are marked. It should be noted that *še-* requires no phonetic change, consequently, it has a low rate of deviations (only vowel deletion occurs, a result of the fast-speech phenomenon). The *ha-* also requires only one phonetic change (into *he-*). This pronunciation is almost always overlooked and actualized as the unmarked *ha-*.

Thus, the more changes required in various environments for a given prefixed particle, both in the prefixed vowel and in the initial syllable, the more marked are the changes; and the more marked the changes, the more are they neutralized with the unmarked forms.

5.3 Naturalness in Phonetic Terms

The marked rules are unnatural in another respect. As mentioned previously, the environments for the rule can be stated in part in phonetic terms, but there is no way whatsoever to avoid stating the vocalization (punctuation) system. The rules are formalized with relation to "shewa mobile," "compound shewas," the "guttural" ', *h,* *ḥ, ',* and other letters (not phonemes), e.g., *k* is spirantized when spelled as "kaf" and not when spelled as "qof". Every speaker finds it extremely complicated to think of orthography and vocalization in his natural speech; no one is capable of constant spelling pronunciation.

5.4 Phonological Justification

As mentioned in section 4.4, most of the errors showed pronunciation as the unmarked, base form, with no change in the words to which the particles are attached. [17] These two results have a double impact - a phonological one and a syntactic one (see 5.5, below). From a phonological point of view, the processes which occurred here, namely the direction of the error, point toward the process of neutralization. The opposition between the unmarked forms (environment E in Table 1), and the marked forms (environments A-D in Table 1) is cancelled, unmarked forms take over the marked ones, and the marked forms are neutralized.

In general, the process of neutralization [18] is common where oppositions exist between two forms, one of which is phonologically and morphologically marked, i.e., more complicated than the other (see Troubetzkoy, 1936, pp. 29-45). In the case of prefixed

[16] Since the rule for assigning *va-* (environment D) is restricted to several compounds of opposite nature, I did not formulate the rule here. The *va-* occurs before stressed syllables in compounds such as *yom valayla, kayic vaḥoref, 'or vaḥosex* 'day and night, summer and winter, light and dark.'
[17] We ignore the fast-speech phenomena (see footnote 13).
[18] This process is commonly referred to as analogy (Bloomfield, 1933, pp. 404-424, Anttila, 1977) or simplification (King, 1969, pp. 58-134).

particles, the unmarked forms are simpler and more frequently used, whereas the other forms are rare and complicated as far as statement of the rules and application of the morphophonemic features are concerned. Therefore, the opposition between the forms is cancelled and the marked forms are neutralized with the unmarked forms.

5.5 Morphosyntactic Justification

The prefixation of the particles requires the application of morphophonemic rules, primarily the spirantization rule which changes *p b k* into *f v x* in environments A, D, and E (see comment (4)), and shewa deletion in environments A, C, and E. Most of the deviations show that the spirantization rule is extremely unproductive, as argued on independent groupds (Schwarzwald, 1976[19]). The same is true for the shewa dele-tion. The deletion is common in fast-speech, but not in formal, slowly pronounced utterances.

From a morphosyntactic point of view, it seems that the prefixed particles are per-ceived as independent particles, "To" is expressed by *'el* and *lə-*; "in", by *bətox* or *bə-*; "by" by *'al yəde* or *bə-*; "as," by *kəmo* or *kə-*, etc. Since there is no morpho-phonemic change in *'el, bətox, 'al yəde,* and *kəmo* when preceding a noun, the pre-fixed particles analogously do not alternate in the appropriate environment. The independent particles do not interfere with the phonological structure occurring in the next word, and this tendency is generalized to the prefixed particles, which do not cause any changes in words which they precede. It is worth mentioning that the pre-fixed particles in our study were not always phonetically connected to the following words. On numerous occasions there was a pause between the particle and its follower, as in the case of the independent particles, e.g., *ve paːm* 'and once,' *mi yeladim* 'from children.'

5.6 Diachronic Change Vs. Natural Rules

Finally, another comment on the phonetic naturalness of the process involved in the realization of the prefixed particles. The formal processes and normative rules were appropriate in BH, where *v* was pronounced as *w*, where there was a distinction between *k* and *q*, ' and ', *ḥ* and *x* where the shewa was a short mid-central vowel and where there existed seven distinct vowels *(i eɛ a ' o u)*. Since the phonological struc-ture in MH has changed (*v* stands for BH *w* and *b*, *k* stands for both *k* and *q*, ' and ' are generally pronounced as ', and *ḥ* and *x* as *x*, shewa is *e*, and there are only five distinct vowels: *i e a o u*), the justification for the rules can no longer be explained in natural phonetic terms.

---

[19] The same is true for other language periods and oral traditions of Hebrew. See page 216 and the references cited in the footnotes there.

6. REGISTERS AND MORPHOPHONEMICS

The term "register" in linguistics refers to the type of language used by a given speaker in a particular set of circumstances or contexts (see Halliday et al., 1964, pp. 87-98; Gregory, 1967, pp. 177-198). So far it has been argued that different registers vary in syntactic and lexical features. In other words, the linguistic method by which one could distinguish between several registers employs the use of sentence structure and choice of different lexemes.

The data obtained in this study point to the fact that morphophonemic evidence provides another linguistic criterion for the distinction between registers of speech. The pronunciation of the prefixed particle adds evidence for the characterization of different registers. The more formal the speech, the more are the speakers exacting about the pronunciation of the prefixed particles. We were able to observe the differences between the subjects, where the announcers, who use the most formal speech, have the most accurate expression of the prefixed pronunciation, whereas journalists and students in fairly informal situations have a relatively high rate of deviations.

The justification for the use of this criterion is further supported by observation of natural speech behavior. The layman uses certain linguistic features in his ordinary speech and other features in a more formal situation. In a formal speech he uses complex sentence structures and a highly literary vocabulary. He also tries to be as accurate as possible in his pronunciation of the prefixed particles, but being unaware of the proper environment, for the reasons discussed above, he created awkward hypercorrections, e.g., *he'amur*[20] 'that which was said,' for *ha'amur, uliladim* 'and to children,' for *veliladim, bexol ram* 'loudly, in a loud voice,' for BH *bəqol rām, ḥayalim uxcinim* 'soldiers and officers,' for BH *ḥayyālim uqṣinim*.

BIBLIOGRAPHY

Anttila, R.
  1977   *Analogy.* The Hague and Paris.
Berman (Aronson), R.
  1978   *Modern Hebrew Structure.* Tel Aviv.
Bloomfield, L.
  1933   *Language.* New York.
Bolozky, S.
  1977   "Fast Speech as a Function of Tempo in Natural Generative Phonology." *Journal of Linguistics* 13:217-238.

---

[20] As a matter of fact, this form occurs in some prayer books. However, I doubt if those who pronounce the hypercorrected forms are aware of the liturgical use.

Gesenius, W.

    1910   *Hebrew Grammar.* E. Kautzsch (ed.). A. E. Cowley (trans.), Oxford.

Gottstein, M., Z. Lievne, and S. Span

    1954   *hadiqduq ha'ivri hašimuši.* Tel Aviv.

Gregory, M.

    1967   "Aspects of Varieties Differentiation." *Journal of Linguistics,* 3:177-198.

Halliday, M.A.K., A. McIntosh, and P. Strevens

    1964   *The Linguistic Sciences and Language Teaching,* London.

King, R. D.

    1969   *Historical Linguistics and Generative Grammar.* New Jersey.

Schwarzwald, O.

    1976   "Gišot te'oretiyot qonqretiyot umufšatot lənituaḥ BGDKPT-BKP bə'ivrit." *Lešonénu,* 40:211-232.

Troubetzkoy, N.S.

    1936   "Die Aufhebung der phonologischen Gegensätze." *Travaux du Cercle Linguistique de Prague* VI: 29-45.

Monographic Journals of the Near East　　　*Afroasiatic Linguistics* 9/2 (June, 1984)

ANALOGY AND REGULARIZATION IN MORPHOPHONEMIC CHANGES: THE CASE OF THE WEAK VERBS IN POST-BIBLICAL AND COLLOQUIAL MODERN HEBREW

by

Ora Rodrigue Schwarzwald

Bar-Ilan University, Israel

Both Post-Biblical Hebrew and Modern Hebrew deviate from Biblical Hebrew in the weak verb morphophonemics. The deviations demonstrate parallel changes. On the one hand, there is a strong analogy between phonetic two-consonantal-root paradigms and between verbs with final vowels. On the other hand, there is a tendency to regularize weak roots by conjugating them as strong verbs. The changes call for a different classification of the root system in Modern Hebrew.

Table of Contents

1. INTRODUCTION

Language is dynamic. It fluctuates constantly and it changes among speakers in various situations and time periods. In the Hebrew language, there is a specific grammatical area which displays such a change during two distinct periods of its history. This area is that of the weak verb, which is the topic of the present discussion.

Hebrew is an ancient language, the Bible being the largest written document existing from its earliest stages. The Bible reflects the language used thousands of years ago, known as Biblical Hebrew (BH).[1] Post-Biblical Hebrew (PBH, i.e., Mishnaic Hebrew) represents a different stage of the language. It is documented in numerous writings, such as the Mishna, collections of legends and rules, etc. PBH is the successor of BH, and was spoken by the Israelites in Palestine until about 200 A.D., when the Aramaic language took over. Comparison of the variations in the weak verbs as used during these two periods shows several linguistic changes.

Modern Hebrew (MH) has been spoken in Palestine (later Israel) since the beginning of this century. It became a living language after having been used as an almost exclusively literary language, primarily for religious ritual use, for 2,000 years. The morphology of BH was set as the normative standard of MH. However, in the speech of native speakers today there are many deviations, which can be considered as changes from the BH norms. In the case of the weak verbs, we note that many of the processes which are occurring in MH are a repetition of processes which took place thousands of years ago. We shall demonstrate that the differences between BH and PBH, and between BH and MH, are not accidental, but follow a pattern caused by the phonetic similarity of the verbs, the opacity of the roots, the inability of the speakers to set the phonological roots analytically apart, and the tendency towards regularization in the verbal system.

---

[1] Although there are variations in BH ranging from archaic forms in poetry to relatively late forms of the Second Temple period, we shall refer here by BH to the phenomena occurring in the early Biblical Prose.

1.1 An Introductory Sketch of Hebrew Morphology

It is well known that in Hebrew morphology, as well as in other Semitic languages, most of the words include two morphs: a consonantal root and a pattern. All verbs, without exception, are formed by combining a specific set of vowels - with or without affixes (i.e., the patterns)[2] - with the root, to make the base form to which the inflectional affixes will be added. For example, the roots *k-š-r* and *š-l-m*, with various patterns, represent different verbs in MH, as shown in (1).[3]

(1) *kašar* 'tied' *(k-š-r+-a-a-,* pattern *pa'al), nikšar* 'was tied' *(k-š-r+ni-a-,* pattern *nif'al), kišer* 'connected' *(k-š-r+-i-e-,* pattern *pi'el), kušar* 'was connected' *(k-š-r+-u-a-,* pattern *pu'al), hitkašer* 'contacted' *(k-š-r+hit-a-e-,* pattern *hitpa'el).*
nišlam 'completed' *(š-l-m+ni-a-,* pattern *nif'al), šilem* 'paid' *(š-l-m+-i-e-,* pattern *pi'el), šulam* 'was paid' *(š-l-m+-u-a-,* pattern *pu'al), hištalem* 'was worthwhile' *(š-l-m+hit-a-e-,* pattern *hitpa'el),*[4] *hišlim* 'completed' *(š-l-m+hi-i-,* pattern *hif-il), hušlam* 'was completed' *(š-l-m+hu-a-,* pattern *huf'al).*

Although most of the roots include three consonants, there are a few which have four and, rarely, five. These take only patterns of the form *-i-e, -u-a-, hit-a-e-,* i.e., *pi'el, pu'al,* and *hitpa'el,*[5] e.g., *t-l-g-r-f, tilgref* 'cabled,' *p-s-t-r, pustar* 'was pasteurized,' *'-k-l-m, hit'aklem* 'became acclimatized.'

1.2 The Weak Verb

There is a large group of verbs to which three consonantal roots are attributed, although phonetically and morphologically in most cases only two consonants show up. These are the weak verbs which will be our primary interest in this paper.

Table 1 illustrates the variations in the conjugation of various roots in normative MH. All the verbs occur in the third person singular form. *Pkd* (a) is a strong root, the rest (b-h) are weak. The prefix *y*+ is the future third person singular marker. The consonantal roots are underlined. (Compare to the BH forms presented in (2)).

---

[2] In BH and PBH, gemination was also a pattern marker. See Fn. 5. It will be marked below as a double consonant, although it is presumably a longer single consonant.
[3] Incidentally, not all the patterns occur with any root. Various restrictions prevent the roots from co-occurring with certain patterns.
[4] There is a metathesis in this pattern when the first radical is a sibilant, therefore, *hitšalem>hištalem.*
[5] In BH: *pi'el, pu'al, hitpa'el* occur with a medial geminate consonant, thus the BH relevant forms in (1) are: *qiššer, quššar, hitqaššer, šillem, šullam hištallem.* Gemination was lost in MH, and /q/ was neutralized into /k/.

TABLE 1
Examples of Strong and Weak Verb Formations
in Normative MH

Verb Type		a	b	c	d	e	f	g	h	i
Root		PKD	NPL	YRŠ	YSB	'KL	SBB	MWT	KR'	KNY
pa'al	past	pakad	nafal	yaraš	yašav	'axal	savav	met	kara	kana
pa'al	future	yifkod	yipol	yiraš	yešev	yoxal	yasov	yamut	yikra	yikne
hif'il	past	hifkid	hipil	horiš	hošiv	he'exil	hesev	hemit	hikri	hikna
hif'il	future	yafkid	yapil	yoriš	yošiv	ya'axil	yasev	yamit	yakri	yakne
pa'al	gloss	'order'	'fall'	'inherit'	'sit'	'eat'	'encircle'	'die'	'read'	'buy'
hif'il	gloss	'deposit with'	'drop'	'bequeath'	'seat'	'feed'	'surround'	'kill'	'read out'	'hand over'

1.2.1　Classification I

The weak verbs are traditionally classified (Gesenius 1910: 118)[6] into two groups, according to the processes which they undergo:

(a)　those roots in which a radical (root consonant) is entirely assimilated (deleted in MH, see footnote 5) and which resemble the strong regular verbs (as in (b-c) in table 1 and in (2)).

(b)　those roots with a semivowel instead of a consonant, in which there is a vowel change, and the verbal forms deviate from the regular forms quite remarkably (as in (d-i) in table 1 and in (2)).

The examples in (2) compare the regular, strong form (2a) to the weak ones (2b-i) in Biblical Hebrew in the *pa'al* future tense.

(2)　a. *yiqšor* 'will tie' (q-š-r)　　　　f. *yāsov* 'will turn' (s-b-b)[7]
　　　b. *yippol* 'will fall' (n-p-l)　　　　g. *yāmuṭ* 'will die' (m-w-t)
　　　c. *yiraš* 'will inherit' (w-r-š)　　　h. *yiqrā* 'will read' (q-r-')
　　　d. *yēšēv* 'will sit' (w-š-b)　　　　i. *yiqrɛ* 'will happen' (q-r-y)
　　　e. *yoxal* 'will eat' ('-k-l)

The examples in (2a-c) are historically derived from *yaqšuru, *yanpulu, *yawrašu through series of phonological rules such as a>i, u>ϕ, u>o, nC>CC, w>y (for details of conditions and justification see Bauer and Leander 1962: 189-200, 300-301). They could also be synchronically motivated in BH as being derived from /yaqšor, yanpol,

---

[6]Gesenius (1910) and Bergsträsser (1918) deal with BH, but since MH morphology is essentially based on BH, this classification is relevant here.
[7]In BH there is a complementary distribution of [pbtdkg] and [fvtdxg]. In MH there are morphophonemic alternations of p∿f, b∿v, k∿x in the verbal system (see Rosen 1977: 63-65).

yayraš/. The examples in (2d-i) can be diachronically motivated by additional series of phonological rules, although some of the forms, such as (2g) and (2f) pose a difficulty in any effort to make them look like natural phonological rules (Brockelmann 1961: 605 ff.). These forms (d-i) can synchronically be taken care of only by morphological rules.

1.2.2 Classification II

A different method of classification groups the weak verbs into three classes, according to the place of radicals in which the change occurs (Bergsträsser 1918: 119-170):

(a) first weak radical:
 I. verbs with initial /'/ (2e)
 II.   verbs with initial /n/ (2b)
 III. verbs with initial /w-y/ (2c-d);
(b) second weak radical:
 I. geminates (2f)
 II.   verbs with medial /w-y/ (2g);
(c) third weak radical:
 I. verbs with final /'/ (2h)
 II.   verbs with final /w-y/ (2i).

This classification takes into account only the place and not the kind of change.

2. THE CHANGES

Two systematic phenomena are common to the changes from BH which occurred in both PBH and MH:

a.   There is a strong analogy between certain verb classes; i.e., there are interminglings of the conjugations of verbs with initial /n/, /w-y/, and medial /w-y/ on the one hand, and of verbs with final /'/ and /w-y/ on the other.

b.   Most of the new roots are conjugated as strong verbs, namely, all the radicals are pronounced.

We shall ignore here other differences, interesting as they may be,[8] and focus our attention on describing and explaining the two phenomena mentioned above, in which the parallel development happened.

---

[8] Other changes typify each of the language periods. For further details see Schwarzwald (1980b). They are explained for PBH as being due to Aramaic influence, simplification of the morphological system, or as a contamination from a Biblical dialect which was slightly different from the standard language presented in the Bible. In MH the differences are explained as being the result of the time discrepancy from BH and of the lack of proper knowledge of the speakers who failed to acquire the normative rules set according to BH.

2.1 Analogy

Analogy - initiated by the Greeks - referred originally to mathematical proportions, but later it was implied by linguists to relations of similarity among linguistic units (Dinneen 1968: 98-99, Anttila 1977: 1-6). The term was widely used by pre-trans-formational grammarians to account for various linguistic changes. Transformational linguists avoided the term in the 1960's and replaced it by other terms such as rule generalization, rule loss and rule ordering, all of which were classified under the title of simplification (King 1969: 58-63, 127-134). However, in the late 1960's and the 1970's few linguists restored the original use of analogy and placed it back in its proper place (e.g., Dinneen 1968: 98-103, Vennemann 1972: 183-204, Anttila 1977).

Analogy as morphological and syntactic process is active in any language. It assimilates one morphological form or syntactic structure into another because of some resem-blance which can be found in their structure. Although analogy is irregular in its occurrence, namely, it is hard to predict its rate and direction of affecting the forms, it causes regularity in the forms being affected (Malone 1969: 534-537). The phonetic structure may cause analogical change, that is, the resemblance in the phonetic forms of different morphemes leads to a similar morphological patterning. Analogy, in turn, may cause phonetic changes in the morphemes (Bloomfield 1933: 404-424). Put differently, analogy is the process by which, due to partly similar phonetic forms in two paradigms (or more), the whole paradigms resemble each other.

In our particular case, analogy denotes the process in which etymologically distinct verbs take the same phonetic output, namely, they share a common morphological conjugation, because of the resemblance which can be found in some phonetic forms of the same morphological paradigm. In other words, two different verbs of various root classes conjugated in the same pattern (morphological paradigm) might participate in a mixed conjugation, where the etymological source is no longer recognized. It is interesting, however, that analogy occurred in both periods of Hebrew independently in the same directions, although not always affecting the same verbs.

2.1.1 Weak Verbs with Initial n, w/y, Medial w/y, and Geminates in BH

In verbs with initial /n/ we find in BH morphophonemic alternations in patterns *pa'al* and *nif'al* between three and two consonantal roots, as in (3).

> (3) *nàfal - yippol* 'fell - will fall' *(n-p-l+pa'al; nafal-yipol in MH), nissal*[9] - *yinnasel* 'was saved - will be saved' *(n-s-l+nif'al; nical-yinacel in MH)*.

The radical /n/ shows up in the *pa'al* past (and present) tense, in *nif'al* future tense, but it is absent in the *pa'al* future and *nif'al* past and present. Compare the strong forms: *šàvar-yišbor, nišbar - yiššàver* 'broke - will break, was broken - will be broken' (š-b-r).

---

[9] The initial *n* here and below is the pattern *nif'al* formative, see (1).

In patterns *hif'il* and *huf'al* there are no morphophonemic alternations. The phonetic root includes only two consonants *(ṣl, kr, pl)*, as in (4).

(4) *hiṣṣil, makkir, yuppal* 'saved, knows, will be dropped' (n-ṣ-l, n-k-r, n-p-l; *hicil, makir, yupal* in formal MH), cf., *hišlim, mašlim, yušlam* in (1).

Thus many of these verbal forms include only two consonantal roots. The same is true for some other verb-classes. In verbs with initial /w-y/, the consonantal /y/ or /w/ always occurs in patterns *pi'el, pu'al* or *hitpa'el* (as the initial /n/ in these patterns). There are morphophonemic alternations in patterns *pa'al* and *nif'al*, where three consonantal roots show up in some forms and only two in others, as in (5). The morphological conditions are the same as in (3) above.

(5) *yāṣav - yeṣev* 'sat - will sit' *(w-š-b*+pa'al; *yašav, yešev* in MH),
    noldā - tiwwāled 'she was born - she will be born' *(w-l-d*+nif'al;
    nolda - tivaled in MH), cf., *šāvar-yišbor, nišbar-yiššāver* in (3).

However, in patterns *hif'il* and *huf'al* there are no morphophonemic alternations. The missing radical shows up in a vowel, but the consonantal root includes only two elements (v-1), as in (6).

(6) *hovil, huval* 'led, was led' (w-b-l), cf., *hišlim hušlam* in (1).

Verbs with medial /w-y/ show no morphophonemic alternations between the three consonants in patterns *pa'al, nif'al, hif'il,* and *huf'al,* such as *q-m, x-n* in (7).[10]

(7) *qām (kam* in MH), *nāxon, hēxin, huxan* 'woke up, true, prepared, was prepared' (q-w-m, k-w-n), cf., *šāvar, nišbar, hišlim, hušlam* (3,4).

A similar situation exists in the case of the geminates.

2.1.2 Changes in PBH

The analogy between these weak verb-classes in both PBH [11] and MH is particularly remarkable in patterns *hif'il* and *huf'al,* in which only two consonantal roots are clearly recognized, and there are no morphophonemic alternations which might indicate the missing third radical of the root. The following examples demonstrate that due to the phonetic output, where only two radicals show up - changes in the morphological paradigms do occur in PBH and MH (see 2.1.3).

In PBH the roots *y-n-q* and *y-ṭ-b* (with initial /w-y/), for instance, are formed in *hif'il* as verbs with medial /w-y/, i.e., as if they were *n-y-q* or *ṭ-w-b* roots, as in (8).

(8) *maniqa, məṭivim* 'suckles (f), do good (pl.), cf., *mēniqa, mēṭivim* in BH.

[10] As for the conjugation in *pi'el, pu'al, hitpa'el,* see section 2.2. It is worth mentioning here that the *huf'al* of first and medial radical (w-y) is identical in BH. Therefore, *huf'al* will be included in our further discussion but without examples.
[11] Based on reliable manuscripts, as described in Haneman (1980) and Schwarzwald (1969).

Verbs with medial /w-y/ are formed analogously to verbs with initial /n/, as in (9).

(9) *hiṭṭil* 'threw' *(t-w-l),* as *hippil* 'dropped' *(n-p-l),* and not as *hēxin* 'prepared,' cf. (7).

The root *b-y-n* in PBH is conjugated as verbs with initial /w-y/, i.e., *'ovin* 'I will explain' as *'ovil* 'I will carry' (w-b-l), and not as BH *'āvin.*

2.1.3 Changes in MH

In MH too, those forms with initial /n/ in *hif'il* and *huf'al,* where the /n/ does not occur phonetically, are commonly pronounced as verbs with medial /w-y/, as in (10).

(10) *hekir, hepil, mepil* 'knew, dropped, drops' *(n-k-r, n-p-l),* as *hexin, mexin* 'prepared, prepares' *(k-w-n),* and not as BH *hikkir, hippil, mappil.*

On the other hand, roots with medial /w-y/ are formed analogous to verbs with initial /n/, as shown in (11).

(11) *macik, mariaḥ* 'annoys, smell' *(c-w-k, r-y-ḥ),* as *mapil* (without gemination, see (10)), and not as *mēxin.*

The root r-y-k and z-w-l are conjugated almost systematically as verbs with initial /w-y/, e.g., *horik, morik, hozil* 'turned, turns green, cheapened,' as in (6), and not as BH *hēriq, mēriq, hēzil.*

2.1.4 Morphophonemic Similarity

Part of the vowel patterning is mostly similar in these patterns, i.e., the stressed /i/ in patterns *hif'il,* the /u,a/ in patterns *huf'al.* Furthermore, since gemination (double consonant) was lost in MH there is no phonetic indication of the assimilated radical in roots with initial /n/. Also, BH *ā* and *a* *(qamats* and *pataḥ)* are pronounced as *a* in MH and in the Palestinian traditions of PBH, therefore, the resemblance among some of the forms becomes more transparent. Compare BH to PBH and normative MH paradigms in table 2.

The forms marked by the asterisks are very similar except for the root radicals, of course. Those marked by a single asterisk are identical already in BH, hence cause analogy of other forms in PBH and MH. The forms marked by two or three asterisks are similar in PBH or in MH. Resemblance in the pattern vowel *i* occurs in all the other forms as well, and only two consonants of the root are phonetically recognizable in these patterns (p-1, x-n, n-q). Since the etymological third radical of the weak root is opaque, due to the lack of morphophonemic alternations, the speakers treat the verbs invariably. They use the patterns properly, but the verb-classes intermingle.

In spite of the variations in the BH weak verb, analogy is active and productive. Therefore, in PBH *y-ṭ-b* and *y-n-q* are conjugated as verbs with medial /w-y/, while *b-y-n,* on the other hand, is formed as a verb with initial /w-y/. In MH, roots belonging to initial /n/ and to medial /w-y/ are interchangeable *(n-k-r* as *k-w-r, c-w-k* as *n-c-k, r-y-k* as *w-r-k,* etc.).

TABLE 2

Hif'il Forms of *n-p-l* 'drop,' *k-w-n* 'prepare,'
and *y-n-q* 'suckle' in BH, PBH and Formal MH

	BH	PBH	MH
PAST	*hippil* **hēxin* **hēniq*	*hippil* **hexin* **heniq*	*hipil* **hexin* **henik*
PRESENT SG.	*mappil* **mēxin* **mēniq*	*mappil* **mexin* **meniq*	*mapil* **mexin* **menik*
PRESENT PL.	*mappilim* *məxinim* *mēniqim*	*mappilim* *məxinim* *məniqim*	*mapilim* ****mexinim* [12] ****menikim*
FUTURE	*yappil* *yāxin* *yēniq*	*yappil* ***yaxin* ***yaniq*	****yapil* ****yaxin* *yenik*
INFINITIVE	*ləhappil* *ləhāxin* *ləhēniq*	*ləhappil* ***ləhaxin* ***ləhaniq*	****lehapil* ****lehaxin* *lehenik*

In PBH the analogy existed between verbs with initial /n/ and medial /w-y/ not only in patterns *hif'il* and *huf'al,* but also in pattern *nif'al.* he reason is the same - only two consonants are recognized in both verb-classes in the past and present (*(niṣṣal,* 'was saved' (phonetic root ṣ-l: the *ni* is the pattern marker; etymological root n-ṣ-l) *naxon* (future: *yikkon*) 'was ready' (k-w-n). The compound forms *niṣṣol* 'was saved' (n-ṣ-l), *niddon* 'was sentenced' (d-w-n), were formed. Here, probably the future form of *yikkon* had some influence on these composed forms.

2.1.5   Changes in Verbs with Final ' or w/y

Another kind of analogy is found among verbs with final /'/ and /w-y/. In these verb-classes there is phonetic identity in many of the BH forms: *qārā-qānā* 'read-bought' (q-r-', q-n-y; *kara-kana* in MH), *niqrā-niqnā* 'was read - was bought' (*nikra-nikna* in MH), *mallē-qawwē* 'fill up(!) - hope(!)' (m-l-', q-w-y; *male-kave* in MH). If we add to this resemblance the vowel change from BH which occurred in PBH according to Palestinian tradition, and in MH, where Biblical distinction between /e-ɛ/ was cancelled, and there exists only one vowel /e/, many more identical forms are formed: *qore-qone* in PBH, *kore-kone* in MH, but *qore-qonɛ* in BH, 'reads, buys,' (q-r-', q-n-y) *məmalle-məqawwe* in PBH, *memale-mekave* in MH, but *məmallē-məqawwɛ* in BH, 'fills up, hopes' (m-l-', q-w-y).

---

[12] In MH historical e, ɛ, ə (*tsere, segol, schwa*) are all pronounced as *e.*

Moreover, since there is a strong resemblance between the verbal forms, and both have two consonantal radicals always followed by a vowel, verbs with final /w-y/, which are more common, tended to influence the forms with final /'/, and the rest of the forms were similarly shaped. In PBH they formed only one paradigm with a final /w-y/, as in (12), whereas in MH they form a non-distinctive alternating paradigm where final /'/ and final /w-y/ are almost in a free distribution, as in (13).

> (12) *qarinu, qorim, niqre* 'we read (past), read (present), will read' (q-r-'),
> as *qaninu, qonim, niqne* 'buy' (q-n-y), and opposed to BH *qārānu, qor'im niqrā,* etc.

> (13) *militi* 'I filled up' instead of BH *milleti* (m-l-'), *ripa* 'cured' instead of BH *rippē* (r-p-'), *likro* 'to happen,' instead of BH *liqrot* (q-r-y), *niseti* 'I tried' instead of *nissiti* (n-s-y), etc.

2.1.6 Final Remark

It should be noted that in BH there was already a sporadic analogy between the weak verb-classes (gesenius 1910: 219, and Bergsträsser 1918: 170-174). Thus, the process which started in BH continues in a more systematic way in the other language periods independently.

2.2 Strong Verb Formation

We now turn our attention to the strong verb formation. In all respects, the verbal system is the most closed and well-structured of the whole morphological system. Most of the verbs are strong. They include three phonetic radicals, and their paradigm follows a strict conjugation according to the verbal patterns (see (1)).

All the weak verb classes are explained in relation to the strong verbs; that is, they are considered as three consonantal verbs in which one of the radicals is weak or missing. This attitude towards the weak verb is not solely characteristic to grammarians. The speakers' intuitions reflect these facts of grammar. The speakers can analyze the consonantal roots of the verb. Their tendency is to assign three radicals to each verb. The difficulty arises in identifying the proper weak roots. The consonantal radicals are obvious, but the missing elements cause confusion. Therefore, they assign the obvious two radicals for these verbs and they add invariably a weak radical, e.g., *q-w-m, n-q-m, y-q-m, w-q-m, q-m-m* (for *n-q-m;* see Schwarzwald 1980a:63-76).

When new roots come into use in the language, or when new meanings are assigned to existing roots, there is a strong tendency to form them as strong verbs, so that all three radicals are pronounced, rather than as weak ones, where one may have to guess what conjugation they take.

2.2.1 *Pi'el, pu'al* and *hitpa'el*

In BH verbs with medial /w-y/ and geminates take two ways of conjugation in patterns *pi'el, pu'al* and *hitpa'el:*

(a) either the vowels are replaced by the patterns -o-e-, -o-a-, hiṯ-o-e-
     (polel, polal, hiṯpolel), with duplication of the last consonant, as in
     (14) and (16), or

(b) less frequently, they are conjugated as the strong verb, as in (15)
     and (17).

(14) *qomem, qomam, hiṯqomem* 'raised against, was raised against, rose against'
      (q-w-m), cf., *Šillem, Šullam, hištallem.* 'paid, was paid, was worthwhile'
      (š-l-m).

(15) *qiyyem, quyyam, hiṯqayyem* 'maintained, was maintained, was materialized'
      (q-y-m).

(16) *golel, golal, hiṯgolel* 'rolled, was rolled, rolled himself,' *(g-l-l)*.

(17) *liqqeq, luqqaq, hiṯlaqqeq* 'licked, was licked, licked himself' *(l-q-q)*.

In PBH forms such as (15) and (17) are dominant; forms as in (14) and (16) are rare
and used only in citations or ritual forms. In MH the new weak roots which belong
to these verb-classes are also formed as (15) and (17). No new roots are conjugated
like (14) and (16). In other words, patterns *polel, polal* and *hiṯpolel* were abandoned
in favor of the regular strong conjugation.

2.2.2 Additional Strong Conjugations

In addition to roots with medial /w-y/ and geminates that take the strong regular
conjugation, there are many roots in which the initial /n/ is neither assimilated nor
deleted in MH, as can be seen in (18).

(18) *yinbaḥ, yinbat, hinbit, hinpik* 'will bark, will bud (intrans.), budded
      (trans.), issued' *(n-b-ḥ, n-b-t, n-p-k)*, cf., *yiggaš, hippil* 'will approach,
      dropped' in BH *(n-g-š, n-p-l)*.

Also, the root w-r-d is formed as a strong verb, namely *hivrid* 'became pink' as *hišlim*,
instead of *horid* 'brought down.' [13]

Table 3 reveals the actual rate of weak verb conjugations among the new weak roots.
Three hundred and twelve new roots are listed in Barkali (1966:86-88) and the table
shows their distribution. It is obvious that the rate of weak conjugation among the
weak roots is very low.

This trend to form weak root as strong verbs is common to both PBH and MH. Part
of this tendency in PBH is attributed to Aramaic influence, but it seems to us that
this trend could have occurred independently, due to the speaker's wish to normalize
irregular forms and alter them to fit into the existing closed paradigms of the verb.

---

[13]The verb is denominalized from *vered* 'rose,' *varod* 'pink.' The strong formation keeps the consonantal value of the nominal root. Another reason is probably for semantic differentiation.

TABLE 3

Weak vs. Strong Conjugation in New Roots

TYPE OF ROOTS	NUMBER OF ROOTS	STRONG CONJUGATION	WEAK CONJUGATION
Strong Tri-Consonantal	115	115	--
Four Consonantal	95(a)	95	--
Five Consonantal	3(a)	3	--
First /w-y/	8	8	--
First /n/	11	8(+1)(b)	(1+)2
Medial /w-y/	34	30	4
Geminates	19	18	1
Final /'/	5	--	5
Final /w-y/	10	--	10(c)

(a)   Four and five consonantal roots always take *pi'el, pu'al* and *hitpa'el* conjugation. See 1.1.

(b)   One root is conjugated as partly weak, partly strong.

(c)   Eight (!) of these are old roots with new meanings.

3.   IN CONCLUSION

In the present paper we showed that there occurred independently a parallel development of the weak verb from BH in both PBH and in MH. It seems that, in part, these changes are a result of phonetic resemblance among various weak verb classes. Another reason for the changes is the tendency to normalize the weak verbs by forming them as strong verbs.

3.1 Classification III

In light of the changes, it seems obvious that the classifications of the weak verbs made for BH as presented in 1.2 are inadequate for the other language periods. The classification must be revised. Based on morphophonemic alternations we offer to classify the roots into three categories:

(a)   Three-consonantal-roots: the roots in which all the consonants show up in all or in part of the paradigm. Namely, three consonantal roots are those in which at least in part of the conjugation the three radicals are clearly recognized, e.g., pakad-yifkod *(p-k-d)*, nafal-yipol *(n-p-l)*.

(b)   Two-consonantal-roots: the roots in which only two consonants show up in the conjugation, e.g., hetil-yatil (t-l), hikir-yakir (k-r).

(c)   Two-consonants-followed-by-a-vowel-roots: roots which etymologically belong to final /'/ or /w-y/ radicals, and the surface phonetic forms reveal the two consonants followed by the vowel.

With this classification the grammar needs less morphological rules to determine the verbal conjugations (see Schwarzwald 1977). Instead of nine morphological groups of rules to the forms presented in Table 1, only three groups are required. For convenience, I shall repeat here the Table to exemplify the classification: the solid line encircles group (a) of our classification (three-consonantal-roots), the dotted line encircles group (b) (two-consonantal-roots) and the broken line - group (c) (two-consonants-followed-by-a-vowel-roots).

TABLE 1'
Root Classification

VERB TYPE	a	b	c	d	e	f	g	h	i
pa'al	*pakad* *yifkod*	*nafal* *yipol*	*yaraš* *yiraš*	*yašav* *yešev*	*'axal* *yoxal*	*savav* *yasov*	*met* *yamut*	*kara* *yikra*	*kana* *yikne*
hif'il	*hifkid* *yafkid*	*hipil* *yapil*	*horiš* *yoriš*	*hošiv* *yošiv*	*he'exil* *ya'axil*	*hesev* *yasev*	*hemit* *yamit*	*hikri* *yakri*	*hikna* *yakne*

This classification reflects the speaker's use of the language and his knowledge of the roots, it simplifies the lexicon, and finally, it helps us understand the processes which have occurred, and are still occurring in the Hebrew language.

BIBLIOGRAPHY

Anttila, R.
   1977   *Analogy.* The Hague: Mouton.
Barkali, S.
   1966   *luaḥ hape'alim hašalem.* Jerusalem: Reuben Mas.
Bauer, H. and P. Leander
   1962   *Historische Grammatik der Hebräischen Sprache des alten Testamentes.* Hildesheim: George Olms.
Bergsträsser, G.
   1918   *Hebräische Grammatik.* Hildesheim: George Olms.
Bloomfield, L.
   1933   *Language.* New York: Holt, Rinehart and Winston.
Brockelmann, C.
   1961   *Grundriss der vergleichenden Grammatik der semitischen Sprachen.* Hildesheim: George Olms.
Dinneen, F. P.
   1968   Analogy, Langue and Parole. *Lingua* 21, 98-103.
Gesenius, W.
   1910   *Hebrew Grammar.* E. Kautzsch (ed.), A. E. Cowley (trans.), Oxford: Clarendon Press.
Haneman, N. G.
   1980   *torat hacurot šel lešon hamišna.* Tel Aviv: Tel Aviv University.
King, R. D.
   1969   *Historical Linguistics and Generative Grammar.* New Jersey: Prentice Hall.

Malone, J. L.
    1969   Rules of Synchronic Analogy: A Proposal Based on Evidence from Three Semitic
            Languages. *Foundations of Language* 5, 534-559.
Rosen, H. B.
    1977   *Contemporary Hebrew.* The Hague: Mouton.
Schwarzwald, O. R.
    1969   hagzarot haʼalulot bilšon hamišna ʼal pi hamišna mahadurat Lowe. Unpublished M.A.
            thesis. Bar-Ilan University, Ramat-Gan.

    1977   yicugam haleksikali šel hapeʻalim haʼalulim. *Hebrew Computational Linguistics* 12, 25-36.

    1980a   meʻalilot hapoʻal heʻalul. *Balshanut Shimushit* 2, 63-76.

    1980b   tahalixim makbilim bilšon ḥaxamim uvilšon yamenu. *Studies in Hebrew and Semitic
            Languages.* Ramat Gan: Bar-Ilan University.
Vennemann, T.
    1972   Phonetic Analogy and Conceptual Analogy. In T. Vennemann and T. W. Wilbur.
            *Schuchardt, the Neogrammarians, and the Transformational Theory of Phonological
            Change.* Athenäum verlag: Frankfurt/M, 181-204.

Monographic Journals of the Near East   *Afroasiatic Linguistics* 9/2 (June, 1984)

CAUSATIVIZATION AND TRANSITIVIZATION
IN ARABIC AND MODERN HEBREW*

by

George N. Saad and Shmuel Bolozky

University of Massachusetts/Amherst

Syntactically, transitivization entails an increase in the number of arguments of the predicate; semantically, it increases the agentivity of the verb or the affectedness of the patient. Causativization in Arabic and Hebrew is shown to be a transitivization process, which introduces an agentive subject (i.e. increase in arguments, and increase in agentivity), and demotes the original subject to patient (i.e. increase in "patienthood"—though only vacuously when the basic verb is non-active). Morphological causativization and semantic transitivity are essentially mutually exclusive: The more transitive a verb is, the more likely it is to be a basic, non-derived causative (like English *kill*), and thus the least likely to be further transitivized by a morphological transitivization process. The somewhat different causativization strategies of transitive verbs in Arabic and Hebrew are discussed in some detail.

Table of Contents

*This research was supported in part by a grant from the Research Council of the University of Massachusetts, Amherst. It constitutes part of a more general paper, read at the 1980 meeting of the North American Conference on Afro-Asiatic Linguistics, April 13-14, San Francisco. We wish to thank Richard Steiner, Lloyd Anderson, Ruth Berman and Paul Hopper for their useful comments on the fuller version.

1. CAUSATIVIZATION AND TRANSITIVITY

In Saad and Bolozky (1980) we defined causativization in Arabic and Hebrew as a morphological process that has syntactic and semantic consequences; it involves syntactic demotion, and semantic demotion with respect to active but not to non-active verbs. We developed a theory of syntacto-semantic transitivity, the semantic aspect of which corresponds to Hopper and Thompson's (1980) "affectedness of the object". Semantically, verbs whose subjects are agents and whose objects are patients are "most" transitive, and within this class of verbs, some are more transitive than others, as can be seen in the following descending order:

(1) a. *John killed Bill*
    b. *John wounded Bill*
    c. *John beat Bill*
    d. *John hit Bill*

Even one and the same verb can be more transitive in some context than in another. Bolinger (1977) suggests that a genuine transitive relationship between verb and patient is a necessary condition for passivization; a weakly transitive verb-object relationship as in (2) and (3) only marginally allows passivization:

(2) a. *Private Smith deserted the army*
    b. **The army was deserted by Private Smith*

(3) a. *The commander-in-chief deserted the army*
    b. *The army was deserted by the commander-in-chief*

Similarly, Ibn Ya'is (vol. 7, p.73) suggests that THE SOURCE (i.e. an extended cognate object) can become subject of a passive verb only when it is conceived of as being a patient as a result of further specifying the meaning of the verb (see Saad, 1975:121-124). According to our analysis, *desert* is more transitive in (2) than it is in (3) above, since among two-place transitive verbs, the "least" transitive ones are those whose objects are "ranges", like *desert* with respect to *army*. The term "range", borrowed from Halliday (1967) and elaborated upon in Longacre (1976), refers to the semantic role of the nominal that completes or further specifies the activity, experience, or state indicated by the verb. The nearest syntactic term equivalent to range is "cognate object". A cognate object is a highly generic nominal built morphologically on the same root as its corresponding verb (e.g. *sing:song, drink:drink, know:knowledge, compose: composition*). A highly generic nominal closely associated with the meaning of a certain verb, however, need not be cognate with that verb (e.g. *eat:food, play:game, run:race*). Ranges are more specific, and often more concrete, than cognate objects, and although their meanings are closely associated with the meanings of their corresponding verbs, they are more independent of their verbs than cognate objects are. In general, inanimate objects of action verbs like *run, fight, play, dance, sing, eat, drink*, etc. . . ., objects of factitive verbs like *build, make, compose, establish*, etc. . . ., and objects of cognitive verbs like *know, understand, realize, read, study*, etc. . . . have the semantic role range. Our analysis of transitivity predicts that with verbs whose objects are ranges, the more specified and/or concretized the range is, the higher is the verb on the transitivity scale. The following sentencial contexts illustrate a scale of transitivity for the verb *eat* in ascending order.

(4) a. *John ate his food*
    b. *John ate lots of food*

c. *John ate spaghetti*
d. *John ate poisoned spaghetti*

Our concept of transitivity is simpler than Hopper and Thompson's (1980), which proposes ten scalar parameters for transitivity. In our approach, most qualifiers of a verb such as aspect, mode, etc., do not constitute elements of transitivity proper, which we believe should be restricted to two features only, one syntactic, the other semantic: the number of participants involved and the degree of affectedness of the object (or degree of "patienthood"). At least as far as Arabic and Hebrew are concerned, these two are sufficient for the purpose of accounting for all or most morphological processes applying to the verb. It is either the syntactic feature, or the semantic one, or both, reinforcing each other. What it means is that, basically, all morphological verb processes in the two languages may be characterized as transitivization or detransitivization phenomena, manifest in either a change in the number of arguments involved (increase or decrease), or in change in degree of semantic transitivity (strengthening or weakening), or in both.

Thus, causativization is a transitivization process, which increases the number of obligatory arguments of the predicate and strengthens it semantically by introducing an agentive subject, and increases "patienthood" by demoting the original subject to patient (though only vacuously when the basic verb is non-active).

2. CAUSATIVIZATION OF INTRANSITIVE VERBS

Most causative verbs in Arabic and Hebrew are derived from basic intransitive verbs. The derivation of a causative verb from a noncausative intransitive verb involves the demotion of the intransitive subject to a patient object and the introduction of an agentive subject which can be any member of a set of noun phrases that satisfy the selectional restrictions that hold between the causative verb and its subject. In (5) below, Standard Arabic *'aḥzana* "cause to become sad" is morphologically derived from *ḥazina* "become sad",

(5) a. *ḥazina*   *bakr - un*
       'became sad   Bakr - nom.'
       'Bakr became sad'

    b. *'aḥzana*   *zayd - un*   *bakr - an*
       'made sad   Zayd - nom.   Bakr - acc.'
       'Zayd made Bakr sad'

Since the subject in (5a) is not an agent, its semantic demotion to patient is vacuous. But the causativizable intransitive verb need not be non-active. In Arabic (6) below, the intransitive verb is active, and although its subject is not an agent (because its activity does not affect any other participant distinct from itself), it is still an actor. When demoted to object, as in (6b), it is also demoted to patient semantically, as it no longer initiates the activity referred to by the predicate.

(6) a. *raqaṣat*   *hind - un*
       'danced   Hind - nom.'
       'Hind danced'

    b. *'arqaṣa*   *zayd - un*   *Hind - an*
       'made dance   Zayd - nom.   Hind - acc.'
       'Zayd made Hind dance'

It can easily be seen, then, that causativization increases the transitivity of an intransitive verb both syntactically and semantically by "creating" an additional argument which is semantically an agent and by increasing the "patienthood" of the demoted original argument.

3. CAUSATIVIZATION OF TRANSITIVE VERBS

3.1 Semantic and Syntactic Consequences

Causativization of transitive verbs has similar consequences. It involves introduction of an agentive subject, resulting in syntactic demotion from subject to direct object, and from sole direct object to second direct object or oblique object (in Modern Hebrew the latter is commoner). Semantically, it demotes the subject from agent to patient only when the verb is active; semantic demotion of subjects of verbs like Arabic *sami'a* 'hear' (or Hebrew *šama'*) is vacuous. Arabic (7) and (8) below illustrate the point:

(7) a. *sami'a bakr-un   al-'uġniya-ta*
     'heard Bakr-nom. the-song-acc.'
     'Bakr heard the song'

   b. *'asma'a   zayd-un   bakr-an   al-'uġniya-ta*
     'made hear Zayd-nom. Bakr-acc. the-song-acc.'
     'Zayd made Bakr hear the song'

(8) a. *šariba al-ṭifl-u   al-dawā'-a*
     'drank the-child-nom. the-medicine-acc.'
     'The child drank the medicine'

   b. *šarrabat   al-'umm-u   al-ṭifl-a   al-dawā'-a*
     'made drink the-mother-nom. the-child-acc. the-medicine-acc.'
     'The mother made the child drink the medicine'

3.2 Lists of Causativizable Transitive Verbs

As indicated in section 2 above, Arabic and Hebrew adjectives and intransitive one-place verbs are generally causativizable; the number of causativizable transitives in Arabic and Hebrew is very small when compared to the number of causativizable intransitives. The following are fairly detailed though not comprehensive lists of causativizable transitive verbs and their corresponding derived causative verbs in Arabic[1] and Hebrew respectively.

1. The *'af'ala* form is not alive in MODERN Arabic dialects. Some dialects of Najdi Arabic constitute an exception, but even in those, *'af'ala* is not productive today.

I. ARABIC

BASIC TRANSITIVE VERB	DERIVED CAUSATIVE VERB
1. *darasa* 'study'	*darrasa, 'adrasa* 'teach, instruct, make study, dictate'
2. *kataba* 'write'	*kattaba, 'aktaba* 'teach to write, make write, dictate'
3. *qara'a* 'read'	*'aqra'a* 'teach to read, make read'
4. *faqiha* 'comprehend, have knowledge'	*faqqaha, 'afqaha* 'teach'
5. *'alima* 'have knowledge, be informed'	*'allama* 'teach', *'a'lama* 'inform'
6. *ḥafiða* 'memorize'	*ḥaffaða* 'make memorize'
7. *fahima* 'understand'	*fahhama, 'afhama* 'make understand, instruct'
8. *ðakara* 'remember'	*ðakkara, 'aðkara* 'remind'
9. *nasiya* 'forget'	*nassā, 'ansā* 'make forget'
10. *ra'a* 'see'	*'arā* 'make see, show'
11. *sami'a* 'hear'	*samma'a, 'asma'a* 'make hear'
12. *ðāqa* 'taste'	*'aðaqa* 'make taste'
13. *šamma* 'smell'	*šammama, 'ašamma* 'make smell'
14. *massa* 'touch'	*'amassa* 'make touch'
15. *'akala* 'eat'	*'akkala, 'ākala* 'make eat, feed'
16. *laqima* 'eat quickly, gobble'	*laqqama, 'alqama* 'make eat, eat quickly, make gobble'
17. *šariba* 'drink'	*šarraba, 'ašraba* 'make drink, soak'
18. *la'iqa* 'lick'	*la"aqa, 'al'aqa* 'make lick'
19. *maṣṣa* 'suck, absorb'	*'amaṣṣa* 'make suck, make absorb'
20. *labisa* 'wear, put on (a dress or garment)'	*labbasa, 'albasa* 'dress or clothe someone'
21. *raqaṣa* 'dance'	*raqqaṣa, 'arqaṣa* 'make dance'
22. *ḥamala* 'carry'	*ḥammala, 'aḥmala* 'make carry, help carry, load'
23. *ḥafara* 'dig'	*'aḥfara* 'make dig, help dig'
24. *banā* 'build'	*'abnā* 'make build, enable to build'
25. *gazā* 'invade'	*gazzā, 'agzā* 'equip to invade'
26. *zāra* 'visit'	*'azāra* 'make visit'
27. *wariθa* 'inherit'	*warraθa, 'awraθa* 'make inherit, bequest'
28. *waladat* 'give birth (a woman)'	*wallada* 'assist (a woman) in child birth'
29. *malaka* 'possess, own'	*mallaka, 'amlaka* 'make possess, make own'
30. *nakaḥa* 'marry, get married'	*'ankaḥa* 'make marry, give in marriage'
31. *xasira* 'lose (money or property)'	*xassara, 'axsara* 'make lose, cause loss or damage'
32. *rabiḥa* 'gain, profit, win (in sports)'	*rabbaḥa, 'arbaḥa* 'make gain, make profit, make win (in sports)
33. *kasaba* 'earn, gain, win'	*kassaba, 'aksaba* 'make earn, make gain, make win'
34. *tabi'a* 'follow (someone or something)'	*'atba'a* 'make follow someone or something'
35. *bala'a* 'swallow'	*balla'a, 'abla'a* 'make swallow'

II. HEBREW

BASIC TRANSITIVE VERB	DERIVED CAUSATIVE VERB
1. *zaxar* 'remember'	*hizkir* 'make remember, remind'
2. *yaraš* 'inherit'	*horiš* 'make inherit, bequest'
3. *naḥal* 'inherit'	*hinḥil* 'make inherit, bequest'
4. *qana* 'buy, buy knowledge'	*hiqna* 'make know, teach'
5. *šama'* 'hear'	*hišmia'* 'make hear'
6. *yada'* 'know'	*hodia'* 'make know, inform'
7. *ra'a* 'see'	*her'a* 'make see, show'
8. *saxar* 'hire, rent'	*hiśkir* 'make hire, rent'
9. *katav* 'write'	*hixtiv* 'make write, dictate'
10. *šaxaḥ* 'forget'	*hiškiaḥ* 'make forget'
11. *yalad* 'give birth'	*holid* 'make give birth, beget'
12. *safag* 'absorb'	*hispig* 'make absorb'
13. *ṭaraf* 'devour, prey'	*hiṭrif* 'provide, prey, feed'
14. *ḥatam* 'sign'	*heḥtim* 'make sign'
15. *'avar* 'pass'	*he'evir* 'make pass, help cross'
16. *lavaš* 'wear'	*hilbiš* 'make wear, dress someone'
17. *pašaṭ* 'take off (clothes, etc.)'	*hifšiṭ* 'make undress'
18. *raqad* 'dance'	*hirqid* 'make dance'
19. *'axal* 'eat'	*he'exil* 'make eat, feed'
20. *lamad* 'learn'	*limed* 'teach'
21. *qara'* 'read'	*hiqri'* 'make read (Mishnaic), read aloud'
22. *bala'* 'swallow'	*hivlia'* 'make swallow (lit.)'
23. *gama'* 'drink, gulp (lit.)'	*higmia'* 'make drink, gulp (lit.)'
24. *lava* 'borrow'	*hilva* 'lend (for value to be returned)'
25. *ša'al* 'borrow'	*hiš'il* 'lend (for object to be returned)'
26. *naśa'* 'marry (tr.)'	*hiśi'* 'make marry, give in marriage'

We do not claim that the basic transitive verbs listed in I and II are the only causativizable transitive verbs in Arabic and Hebrew. Note the overlap between the two lists. The causativizable transitives glossed in English as *remember, forget, see, hear, know, inherit, write, wear, eat, absorb, dance, give birth, study, read, swallow, drink,* and *marry,* are common to both Arabic and Hebrew.

That transitive verbs are rarely causativized is also supported by neutralization phenomena such as in less normative Hebrew usage today (e.g. *hiśkir* 'rent, tr.', *hilva* 'lend', *hiš'il* 'lend', used causatively as well as for the basic non-causative meaning), and in young children's Hebrew speech (e.g. *hilbiš* 'make wear' and *holid* 'make give birth' for the causative as well as non-causative meaning).

3.3 The Correlation between Causativizability and Semantic Transitivity

The causativizable verbs listed in I and II above can be divided into two groups: active and non-active. In general, non-active transitives have a low degree of transitivity because the semantic role of their subjects is patient rather than agent. The semantic role of the subjects of the active verbs on the lists is agent, but the semantic role of their objects is either goal or range. Active verbs whose objects are goals have a higher degree of transitivity than those whose objects are ranges. The fact that many of these verbs are passivizable is due to contexts in which the objects of these verbs are conceived of as being true affected patients. (See the references to Ibn Ya'īs and Bolinger above.) For example, in sentences like (9) below the (a) passives are more acceptable than the (b) passives because the objects (i.e. the passive subjects) are conceived of as being more affected patients in the (a) sentences than they are in the (b) sentences (for more examples like these see Bolinger 1977).

(9) i. a. *Boston was visited by the Pope last year.*
     b. *Boston was visited by John Smith last year.*
   ii. a. *The Pacific has been sailed by the mightiest fleets in history.*
     b. *The Pacific was sailed by my brother Joe.*

Active transitive verbs that are on the highest end of the transitivity scale involve two distinct participants in the activity indicated by that verb. Almost regardless of context, the subjects of such verbs are semantically causative agents and their objects are affected patients. Examples of verbs like these are the Arabic and Hebrew equivalents of the English verbs *kill, wound, stab, break* and *cut*. Such verbs do not appear on lists I and II because they are not causativizable in Arabic and Hebrew. They are non-derived, basic, causative verbs, and in Arabic and Hebrew, causative verbs, whether basic or derived, are not causativizable. A verb like *kill*, for example, involves two distinct participants; a causative agent (the killer) and an affected patient (the victim). In contrast, a verb like *dance*, which has a very low degree of transitivity, involves one participant only (the dancer). The cognate object of the verb *dance* in a sentence like *The students danced a new dance*, is semantically a range, which is merely a prolongation or further specification of the meaning of the verb itself. While the degree of transitivity of verbs like *dance* and *sing* is context dependent, the degree of transitivity of verbs like *kill* and *break* is independent of context. More significantly, since causation is a strong form of semantic transitivity, morphological causativization is excluded from applying to already-causative lexical transitive verbs. In other words, the more transitive a verb is, the more likely it is to be a basic causative, and thus the least likely to be further transitivized by a morphological causativization process. Thus, the fact that morphological causativization and semantic transitivity are mutually exclusive supports our claim of a correlation between degree of causativity and degree of semantic transitivity.

3.4 Causativization of Transitive Verbs in Arabic

Arabic and Hebrew causative verbs that are derived morphologically from transitive verbs differ in their syntactic behavior.

In Arabic the causativization of a causativizable verb results in a ditransitive verb that takes two accusative objects, as can be seen in (7) and (8) above.

Factors internal to Arabic suggest that the two objects in sentences like (7b) and (8b) above are not only accusative objects but also direct objects: (i) Both are marked accusative; (ii) Either object may follow the subject directly, although in the unmarked word order the derived object precedes the original object; (iii) Either object, but not both, may be advanced to subject by passivization; (iv) When pronominal, either or both objects may be cliticized accusatively to the verb (subjects are cliticized nominatively, and oblique objects may not be cliticized to the verb); (v) Unlike subjects or oblique objects, either object may be topicalized, etc.[2]

2. For further detail on the syntactic nature of the two accusative objects, refer to the following old Arab grammarians: Sībawayhi (Vol. 1), Ibn Ya'īs (Vol. 7), Ibn al-Ḥājib (Vol. 2), and Ibn 'aqīl (Vol. 2).

3.5 Causativization Strategies of Transitive Verbs in Hebrew

In Biblical Hebrew, ditransitive causative verbs behave syntactically more like Arabic ditransitive causatives than their Modern Hebrew counterparts. Thus, while *her'a* 'show', for instance, may take two accusative objects in Biblical Hebrew, it takes only one accusative object in Modern Hebrew, the second object being oblique. The number of verbs that take two accusative objects is considerably more restricted in Modern Hebrew than it is in Biblical Hebrew. This may be an instance of diachronic syntactic change in Hebrew.

In Modern Hebrew there are two causativization strategies of causativizable transitive verbs: One, which is less common and often avoided, entails the occurrence of two accusative objects with the verb, one of which may also be realized obliquely; the other entails a direct object followed by an oblique object, generally the dative *le-* (see Cole 1976). Below is an illustration of the first strategy:

(10) a. *ha-talmidim   raqdu 'et ha-riqud   ha-ḥadaš*
'the-students   danced acc. the-dance   the-new'
'the students danced the new dance'

b. *hirqadeti 'et ha-talmidim*   { *'et ha-riqud* / *ba-riqud* }   *ha-ḥadaš*
'I made dance acc. the-students { acc. the-dance / obl. (in ∿ with)-the-dance } the-new'
'I made the students dance the new dance'

Factors internal to Hebrew suggest the following about the syntactic behavior of objects like the ones in (10b): (i) Both objects may be marked accusative; (ii) The derived object precedes the original object when both objects are definite, but either object may precede the other when the original object is indefinite; (iii) The derived, but not the original, object may be advanced to subject by passivization; (iv) When prenominal, the derived, but not the original, object may be cliticized to the verb; (v) Generally in Hebrew, a resumptive pronoun is optional for relativized direct objects but obligatory for relativized oblique objects. When a derived object, like the one in (10b), is relativized, it must leave behind a resumptive pronoun; a relativized original object may or may not leave behind a pronominal residue.

Unlike the case in Arabic, the first object is "more of a direct object" than the second (cf. Cole 1976) in spite of the fact that the relativization test shows the second object to be "more of a direct object" than the first.

Sentences (10) above illustrate syntactic demotion from subject to direct object as in Arabic, and from sole direct object to second accusative or oblique object. Semantically, causativization of active verbs like *raqad* 'dance' in (10) demotes the subject from agent to patient, but does not affect the object.

Below is an illustration of the (commoner) second strategy:

(11) a. *hu ra'a 'et ha-bayit   ha-ḥadaš šelanu*
'he saw acc. the-house the-new our'
'He saw our new house'

b. *her'eti   lo   'et ha-bayit   ha-ḥadaš šelanu*
'I showed to him acc. the-house the-new   our'
'I showed him our new house'

Sentences like these demonstrate syntactic demotion from subject to object and from sole direct object to oblique object. With non-active verbs like *ra'a* 'see' in (11), the semantic demotion is vacuous. Thus, the active/non-active dichotomy is supported by a difference in semantic demotion: While causativization demotes subjects of active transitive verbs from agent to patient, it does not semantically affect subjects of non-active transitive verbs. And, as observed in Cole (1976), this dichotomy is also supported by the very distribution of causativizable transitive verbs with respect to the two strategies: While active basic verbs tend to follow (10b) when causativized, non-active ones are causativized as in (11b).[3]

4. CONCLUSION

To conclude the discussion of the causativization of transitive verbs, we now return to its characterization as a transitivization phenomenon. Syntactically, transitivization entails an increase in the number of arguments of the predicate; semantically, it increases the agentivity of the verb or the affectedness of the patient. Causativization in Arabic and Hebrew is shown to be a transitivization process, which introduces an agentive subject (i.e. increase in arguments, and increase in agentivity), and demotes the original subject to patient (i.e. increase in 'patienthood'—though only vacuously when the basic verb is non-active). Morphological causativization and semantic transitivity are essentially mutually exclusive.

A broader look at the Arabic and Hebrew data suggests that the phenomenon of causativization is but one of the manifestations of transitivity in the two languages, and that once a larger transitivity framework is assumed, all morphological processes associated with the Semitic verb fall into place. Thus, for instance, formation of comitative verbs in Arabic (form III from form I) is a transitivizing operation in that it adds an accusatively marked argument, forming an initiator-respondent relationship between the subject and that added object. Formation of form II intensives from basic form I verbs does not add an argument, but it increases the affectedness of the objects by intensifying the activity of the verb, either energy-wise or by repetition. On the other hand, morphological passive formation is a manifestation of detransitivization, in that it decreases from the number of arguments (often in Hebrew and obligatorily in Arabic), and while promoting object to subject syntactically, it preserves its semantic role as patient. Reflexivization is also a detransitivization process, in which a subject is lost and the object is promoted to subject, but is still a patient semantically. The formation of attemptive verbs in Arabic (also form III from form I) is an instance of detransitivization as well, involving no loss of argument, but decreasing from the affectedness of the object.

Similar investigation should be conducted of other morphological processes applying in the Arabic and Hebrew verb system, with the purpose of coming up with a complete description and analysis of the processes involved, all in terms of increase or descrease in semantic or syntactic transitivity. Although findings of such research will be restricted to the two languages investigated, they should definitely contribute to the general theory of transitivity; when a language uses a rich morphological apparatus to derive verbs from other verbs, the processes involved will reflect upgrading and downgrading of semantic and syntactic transitivity similar to what happens in Arabic and Hebrew.

---

3. This has led to the proposal by Doron (ms.) that the derivation from (11a) to (11b) go through the intermediate stage of passivization: Sentences like (11b) are closely paralleled by variants in which the original direct object is promoted to subject of a passive participle adjective.

REFERENCES

Bolinger, Dwight
    1977   "Transitivity and spatiality: the passive of prepositional verbs." In A. Makkai et al. (eds),
                   Linguistics at the Crossroads. Padova: Jupiter.

Cole, Peter
    1976   "A causative construction in Modern Hebrew: theoretical implications." *Studies in*
                   Modern Hebrew Syntax and Semantics, ed. by Peter Cole, 99-128. Amsterdam: North
                   Holland.

Doron, Edit.   "Causative via Passive." University of Texas, Austin, ms.

Halliday, M.A.K.
    1967   "Notes on transitivity and theme in English." *Journal of Linguistics* 3:37-81.

Hopper, Paul J. and Thompson, Sandra A.
    1980   "Transitivity in grammar and discourse." *Language* 56, 251-299.

Ibn 'aqīl Bahā' al-Dīn
    1967   *Šarḥ Ibn 'aqīl 'alā 'alfiyyat Ibn Mālik*, 15th ed. Edited by Muḥammad Muḥyī al-Dīn 'abd
                   al-Ḥamīd. Cairo: Dār al-ittiḥād al-'arabī li al-ṭibā'ah.

Ibn al-Ḥājib, Jamāl al-Dīn
    (no date)   *Kitāb al-Kāfiyah fī al-Naḥw.* Edited with commentary by Raḍiyy al-Dīn al-Astarābāði.
                   Beirut: Dār al-Kutub al-'ilmiyyah.

Ibn Ya'īš, Muwaffaq al-Dīn
    (no date)   *Šarḥ al-Mufaṣṣal.* Beirut: 'ālam al-Kutub and Cairo: al-Mutanabbi Library.

Longacre, Robert E.
    1976   *An Anatomy of Speech Notions.* Lisse: The Peter de Ridder Press.

Saad, George N.
    1975   *Transitivity, causation, and the derivation of passives in Arabic.* University of Texas
                   doctoral dissertation.

Saad, George N. and Bolozky, Shmuel
    1980   "Theoretical implications of morphological causativization in Arabic and Hebrew." North
                   American Conference on Afro-Asiatic Linguistics, April 13-14, 1980, San Francisco.

Sībawayhi
    1885   *Kitāb Sībawayhi.* Edited by Hartwig Derenbourg. Paris: L'Imprimerie Nationale.

new from Undena ≋

The Inflection of the Verb in the Pyramid Texts

James P. Allen

This study attempts to uncover, beneath the deficiencies of the hieroglyphic writing system, the identity and morphology of inflected forms of the verb in the earliest well-documented phase of ancient Egyptian. The work complements existing grammatical studies of Old Egyptian in its exclusive concentration on the Pyramid Texts and in its detailed, exhaustive study of the entire verbal system of these texts.

Part 1 examines the complete corpus of written forms extant in the eight known Old Kingdom pyramids (Unis to Pepi II and Pepi II's three queens) and identifies, for each conjugation, the inventory of written forms of the verb. Part 2 analyzes the distribution of these written forms in syntactic environments, in order to identify the morphological paradigms that represent individual inflected forms of the verb. The results of these investigations are summarized in a series of tables. Three appendices to the work contain the basic data on which the study is based, and a bibliography and an index of passages translated and discussed are also provided.

Bibliotheca Aegyptia, Volume 2.   Appr. 785 pages. $56.00 paper, $76.00 cloth

A Dictionary of Nigerian Arabic

Alan S. Kaye

This listing of 6000 lexemes with some illustrative sentences provides material on present Nigerian Arabic studies and gives evidence of a dialect change. This volume English/Nigerian; Nigerian/English volume in preparation.

Bibliotheca Afroasiatica, Volume 1 LC: 81-71736; ISBN: 0-89003-100-2/cloth, 0-89003-101-0/paper Pp. xvi-92; $26.00/cloth, $19.50/paper

In preparation for *BAA* (1984): I. M. Diakonoff *Comparative Historical Vocabulary of Afroasiatic Languages*

Tigre Grammar and Texts

Shlomo Raz

A concise descriptive grammar of the Mansaʿ dialect of the Tigre language, and a selection of new Tigre texts. The author's intention has been to go beyond the existing corpus of texts in order to produce the first comprehensive work in the field. The linguistic material was collected by him during summer 1969 and winter 1970 in Asmara, Massaua and the neighboring areas. The material collected has been as vast as possible, and it reflects the spoken language to a large extent.

Afroasiatic Dialects, Volume 4 LC: 81-71735; ISBN: 0-89003-097-9 Pp. xviii-145; $19.75/paper

ORDER FULFILLMENT: *EISENBRAUNS*, POB 275, Winona Lake, IN 46590, (219) 269-2011. Credit and prepaid order information available.
PUBLISHER: *UNDENA PUBLICATIONS*, POB 97, Malibu, CA 90265, (213) 366-1744. Bibliographic cards, flyers, catalog and order information.